THE ULTIMATE HANDBOOK

VOLUME 2

By Samantha Brooke

SCHOLASTIC INC.

New York Toronto London Auckland Sydney
Mexico City New Delhi Hong Kong Buenos Aires

ISBN-13: 978-0-439-91904-3
ISBN-10: 0-439-91904-5

HASBRO and its logo and LITTLEST PET SHOP are trademarks of Hasbro and are used with permission. © 2007 Hasbro. All Rights Reserved.

Published by Scholastic Inc. under license from HASBRO. SCHOLASTIC and associated logos are trademarks and/or registered trademarks of Scholastic Inc.

12 11 10 9 8 7 6 5 4   7 8 9 10 11/0

Printed in the U.S.A.
First printing, August 2007

TABLE OF CONTENTS

Come on in . . . the temperature's fine!
This pet needs a lot of love
and a special environment where
she can stay warm and cozy.

IGUANA

EYE COLOR: Orange-brown

BODY COLOR: Green

FAVORITE ACCESSORY: Pink carrying case

LIKES: Sunbathing

DISLIKES: Sunburns

FAVORITE FOOD: Sun-dried tomatoes

FAVORITE ACTIVITY: Windsurfing

This pack of dogs is all about fun. A trip to the dog park with these pals is sure to be great!

BOXER

EYE COLOR: Light blue

BODY COLOR: Dark brown and white

FAVORITE ACCESSORY: Comfy bed

LIKES: Afternoon naps

DISLIKES: Bad dreams

FAVORITE FOOD: Herbal tea

FAVORITE ACTIVITY: Dreaming

BOXER

EYE COLOR: Violet

BODY COLOR: White and golden

FAVORITE ACCESSORY: Pink bow

LIKES: Fairy tales

DISLIKES: Animals without manners

FAVORITE FOOD: Tapioca pudding

FAVORITE ACTIVITY: Having tea parties

CHIHUAHUA

EYE COLOR: Lavender

BODY COLOR: Cream and tan

FAVORITE ACCESSORY: Turquoise purse

LIKES: Being tiny

DISLIKES: Almost being stepped on

FAVORITE FOOD: Mini muffins

FAVORITE ACTIVITY: Window-shopping

Some pets like lounging around or napping in the sun, but these adorable pets just can't sit still!

KITTY

EYE COLOR: Blue-green

BODY COLOR: Golden and brown

FAVORITE ACCESSORY: Her pink bottle

LIKES: Using her imagination

DISLIKES: Swimming

FAVORITE FOOD: Jelly beans

FAVORITE ACTIVITY: Riding the seesaw at the playground

SHEEPDOG

EYE COLOR: Bright blue

BODY COLOR: White and gray

FAVORITE ACCESSORY: Her cozy basket

LIKES: Rounding up friends for a game of catch

DISLIKES: Getting hair in her eyes

FAVORITE FOOD: Bacon

FAVORITE ACTIVITY: Having her bangs trimmed

KITTY

EYE COLOR: Pale green

BODY COLOR: Cream and golden

FAVORITE ACCESSORY: Her bottle

LIKES: Lapping up a bowl of yogurt

DISLIKES: Getting sick

FAVORITE FOOD: Mac and cheese

FAVORITE ACTIVITY: Chasing mice

Rain, sleet, or snow can't keep these frisky pets from spending time outside with their buddies!

BEAGLE

EYE COLOR: Dark green

BODY COLOR: Brown and white

FAVORITE ACCESSORY: Deck of cards

LIKES: Winning

DISLIKES: Losing

FAVORITE FOOD: Peanut butter sandwiches

FAVORITE ACTIVITY: Playing "Go Fish"

KITTEN

EYE COLOR: Lavender

BODY COLOR: Cream and white

FAVORITE ACCESSORY: Swing

LIKES: Pretending she can fly

DISLIKES: When recess is over

FAVORITE FOOD: Caramel corn

FAVORITE ACTIVITY: Being pushed on the swing

TURTLE

EYE COLOR: Olive

BODY COLOR: Green

FAVORITE ACCESSORY:
Yoga mat

LIKES: Stretching

DISLIKES: Stiff muscles

FAVORITE FOOD: Chai tea

FAVORITE ACTIVITY: Pilates

TOUCAN

EYE COLOR: Grassy green

BODY COLOR: Pink and yellow

FAVORITE ACCESSORY:
Palm tree perch

LIKES: Dance music

DISLIKES: Sad songs

FAVORITE FOOD:
Pineapple upside-down cake

FAVORITE ACTIVITY: Salsa dancing

BIRD

EYE COLOR: Pale blue

BODY COLOR: Bright red

FAVORITE ACCESSORY:

Feather boa

LIKES: Flapping

DISLIKES: Getting lost

FAVORITE FOOD: Gummy worms

FAVORITE ACTIVITY: Making nests

SQUIRREL

EYE COLOR: Lavender

BODY COLOR: Gray

FAVORITE

ACCESSORY:

Jump rope

LIKES: Cracking nuts

DISLIKES: Winter

FAVORITE FOOD: Pecan pie

FAVORITE ACTIVITY: Hopping from tree to tree

GOLDEN RETRIEVER

EYE COLOR: Light blue

BODY COLOR: White and cream

FAVORITE ACCESSORY:
Pink carrying case

LIKES: Comedies

DISLIKES: Talking during movies

FAVORITE FOOD: Popcorn

FAVORITE ACTIVITY: Watching
movie previews

CHINCHILLA

EYE COLOR: Honey brown

BODY COLOR: Gray and white

FAVORITE ACCESSORY:
Fleece blanket

LIKES: Being soft

DISLIKES: Matted fur

FAVORITE FOOD:
Butter pecan ice cream

FAVORITE ACTIVITY: Cuddling

ST. BERNARD

EYE COLOR: Periwinkle

BODY COLOR: Dark brown, golden brown, and white

FAVORITE ACCESSORY: Snowmobile

LIKES: Licking icicles

DISLIKES: Hot tea

FAVORITE FOOD: Orange Popsicles

FAVORITE ACTIVITY: Making snowballs

FROG

EYE COLOR: Light purple

BODY COLOR: Aquamarine

FAVORITE ACCESSORY: Trampoline

LIKES: Playing hopscotch

DISLIKES: Sitting still

FAVORITE FOOD: Lollipops

FAVORITE ACTIVITY: Sticking out his tongue

COCKER SPANIEL

EYE COLOR: Emerald green

BODY COLOR: Dark brown and white

FAVORITE ACCESSORY: Stopwatch

LIKES: Playing tag

DISLIKES: Getting caught

FAVORITE FOOD: Fruit smoothies

FAVORITE ACTIVITY: Running laps

GUINEA PIG

EYE COLOR: Dark blue

BODY COLOR: Tan and white

FAVORITE ACCESSORY: Board games

LIKES: Rainy days

DISLIKES: Hiking

FAVORITE FOOD: Cheese and crackers

FAVORITE ACTIVITY: Playing checkers

These soft and cuddly pals take their looks—
and relaxation time—very seriously.
After all, they need their beauty rest!

SKUNK

EYE COLOR: Bright blue

BODY COLOR: Black and white

FAVORITE ACCESSORY: Perfume

LIKES: Being spunky

DISLIKES: Licorice

FAVORITE FOOD: Smelly cheese

FAVORITE ACTIVITY: Making a stink

CAT

EYE COLOR: Yellow-green

BODY COLOR: Golden

FAVORITE ACCESSORY: Sweet-smelling flowers

LIKES: Gardening

DISLIKES: Wilted flowers

FAVORITE FOOD: Sunflower seeds

FAVORITE ACTIVITY: Pulling up weeds

CAT

EYE COLOR: Yellow-green

BODY COLOR: White and charcoal

FAVORITE ACCESSORY: Sleeping mask

LIKES: Relaxing in bed

DISLIKES: Alarm clocks

FAVORITE FOOD: Chamomile tea

FAVORITE ACTIVITY: Daydreaming

POODLE

EYE COLOR: Light purple

BODY COLOR: White

FAVORITE ACCESSORY: Diamond collar

LIKES: Being fluffy

DISLIKES: Rainy days

FAVORITE FOOD: Wedding cake

FAVORITE ACTIVITY: Playing croquet

BUNNY

EYE COLOR: Bright blue

BODY COLOR: White

FAVORITE ACCESSORY: Bracelets

LIKES: Swinging in a hammock

DISLIKES: Scary movies

FAVORITE FOOD: Carrot juice

FAVORITE ACTIVITY: Nibbling

PUSH 'N' PLAY

Where do these animals get all that energy? When most of us are ready for bed, these pets are ready to play another game and spend some quality time with YOU!

MONKEY

EYE COLOR: Dark blue

BODY COLOR: Tan and brown

FAVORITE ACCESSORY:
Yo-yo

LIKES: Swinging

DISLIKES: Walking

FAVORITE FOOD: Banana bread

FAVORITE ACTIVITY: Acrobatics

HAMSTER

EYE COLOR: Turquoise

BODY COLOR:
Golden and white

FAVORITE ACCESSORY:
Trail map

LIKES: Hiking

DISLIKES: Getting lost in the woods

FAVORITE FOOD: Trail mix

FAVORITE ACTIVITY: Seeing nature

KITTY

EYE COLOR: Light blue

BODY COLOR: White and charcoal

FAVORITE ACCESSORY: Floral perfume

LIKES: Daffodils

DISLIKES: Insects

FAVORITE FOOD: Rose tea

FAVORITE ACTIVITY: Picking flowers

Aside from needing lots of love and care, your little pal needs baths and trips to the doctor, too. Remember: A healthy pet is a happy pet!

COCKER SPANIEL

EYE COLOR: Light blue

BODY COLOR: Cream

FAVORITE ACCESSORY:
Newspaper

LIKES: Roller coasters

DISLIKES: Long lines

FAVORITE FOOD: Vegetable sticks

FAVORITE ACTIVITY: Meeting other doggies

DOBERMAN

EYE COLOR: Warm brown

BODY COLOR: Black and brown

FAVORITE ACCESSORY:
Fire hydrant

LIKES: Being rewarded with treats

DISLIKES: Horror films

FAVORITE FOOD: Beef stew

FAVORITE ACTIVITY: Barking

KITTY

EYE COLOR: Lime green

BODY COLOR: Golden

FAVORITE ACCESSORY:
Medical bag

LIKES: Being taken care of

DISLIKES: Getting boo-boos

FAVORITE FOOD: Chicken soup

FAVORITE ACTIVITY: Recuperating

GERMAN SHEPHERD

EYE COLOR: Light purple

BODY COLOR: Brown, white, and charcoal

FAVORITE ACCESSORY: Remote
control

LIKES: Cable television

DISLIKES: Breaking bones

FAVORITE FOOD: Breakfast in bed

FAVORITE ACTIVITY: Watching old movies

MOUSE

EYE COLOR: Honey

BODY COLOR: Gray

FAVORITE ACCESSORY:
Anything that can be nibbled

LIKES: Scurrying

DISLIKES: Being bored

FAVORITE FOOD: Cheese fries

FAVORITE ACTIVITY: Playing laser tag

RAT

EYE COLOR: Cotton-candy pink

BODY COLOR: Tan and charcoal

FAVORITE ACCESSORY:
The funny pages

LIKES: Amusement parks

DISLIKES: Water parks

FAVORITE FOOD:
Roast beef sandwiches

FAVORITE ACTIVITY:
Playing chess

CHOW CHOW

EYE COLOR: Blue-gray

BODY COLOR: Golden brown

FAVORITE ACCESSORY:
Bubble bath

LIKES: Getting clean

DISLIKES: Dirt

FAVORITE FOOD: Butterscotch pudding

FAVORITE ACTIVITY: Splashing around

BOXER

EYE COLOR: Forest green

BODY COLOR: Brown and white

FAVORITE ACCESSORY:
Bathtub

LIKES: Rubber duckies

DISLIKES: Having his ears cleaned

FAVORITE FOOD: Swiss cheese

FAVORITE ACTIVITY: Dog-paddling

LONG-HAIRED CAT

EYE COLOR: Turquoise

BODY COLOR: Cream and white

FAVORITE ACCESSORY: Magnifying glass

LIKES: Mysteries

DISLIKES: Hints

FAVORITE FOOD: Fortune cookies

FAVORITE ACTIVITY: Watching James Bond movies

FISH

EYE COLOR: Yellow-green

BODY COLOR: Orange with white stripes

FAVORITE ACCESSORY: Aquarium

LIKES: Blowing bubbles

DISLIKES: Sharks

FAVORITE FOOD: Cucumber sushi

FAVORITE ACTIVITY: Swimming laps

CAT

EYE COLOR: Dark brown

BODY COLOR: Gray

FAVORITE ACCESSORY:
Passport

LIKES: Traveling to new places

DISLIKES: Sitting at home

FAVORITE FOOD:
Anything spicy

FAVORITE ACTIVITY:
Being adventurous

SEA HORSE

EYE COLOR: Turquoise

BODY COLOR: Pink, blue, purple, and green

FAVORITE ACCESSORY:
Aquarium

LIKES: Watching the fish swim by

DISLIKES: Coming up for air

FAVORITE FOOD: Anything with salt

FAVORITE ACTIVITY: Diving

TURTLE

EYE COLOR: Lavender

BODY COLOR: Green

FAVORITE ACCESSORY: Shell

LIKES: Moving slowly

DISLIKES: Being told to hurry up

FAVORITE FOOD: Slow-churned ice cream

FAVORITE ACTIVITY: Taking long walks on the beach

DUCK

EYE COLOR: Aquamarine

BODY COLOR: Yellow and orange

FAVORITE ACCESSORY:
Fluffy beach towel

LIKES: Quacking

DISLIKES: Ruffled feathers

FAVORITE FOOD: Key lime pie

FAVORITE ACTIVITY: Waddling

JACK RUSSELL TERRIER

EYE COLOR: Light blue

BODY COLOR: Brown and white

FAVORITE ACCESSORY: Toy boat

LIKES: Country line dancing

DISLIKES: Mosquitoes

FAVORITE FOOD: Toasted marshmallows

FAVORITE ACTIVITY: Camping

Bring out the SPF 45 because summertime is here! You'll be spending a lot of time playing outdoors with these pals. After all, there's nothing like running through the sprinklers on a muggy day!

CHICK

EYE COLOR: Sky blue

BODY COLOR: Yellow

FAVORITE ACCESSORY: Nest

LIKES: Flapping around

DISLIKES: Custard

FAVORITE FOOD: Wheatgrass juice

FAVORITE ACTIVITY: Flying practice

KITTY

EYE COLOR: Grassy green

BODY COLOR: Gray

FAVORITE ACCESSORY:

Neck massager

LIKES: Love poems

DISLIKES: Mean people

FAVORITE FOOD:

French vanilla ice cream

FAVORITE ACTIVITY:

Getting massages

PIG

EYE COLOR: Bright blue

BODY COLOR: Light pink

FAVORITE ACCESSORY:

Pink bow

LIKES: Making mud pies

DISLIKES: Square-dancing

FAVORITE FOOD: Apples

FAVORITE ACTIVITY: Belly dancing

KITTEN

EYE COLOR: Lime green

BODY COLOR: White

FAVORITE ACCESSORY:

Picnic basket

LIKES: Afternoons in the park

DISLIKES: Cloudy days

FAVORITE FOOD: Sardine

sandwiches

FAVORITE ACTIVITY: Spending time

with friends

DUCK

EYE COLOR:

Ocean blue

BODY COLOR:

White and yellow

FAVORITE ACCESSORY:

Sunglasses

LIKES: The high diving board

DISLIKES: Cloudy days

FAVORITE FOOD: Fried clam strips

FAVORITE ACTIVITY: Building sand castles

JACK RUSSELL TERRIER

EYE COLOR: Orange-brown

BODY COLOR: Tan

FAVORITE ACCESSORY:

Sun hat

LIKES: Digging in the sand

DISLIKES: Sunburns

FAVORITE FOOD: Ice pops

FAVORITE ACTIVITY:

Wakeboarding

CAT

EYE COLOR: Lime green

BODY COLOR: Golden

FAVORITE ACCESSORY: Visor

LIKES: Reading magazines

DISLIKES: Sun in her eyes

FAVORITE FOOD: Oysters on the half shell

FAVORITE ACTIVITY: Beach volleyball

SUPER SASSY

These pets have attitude galore.
They know what they want and how they
want it . . . and what they want
most of all is your love!

BUTTERFLY

EYE COLOR: Blue-green

BODY COLOR:
Purple, pink, and yellow

FAVORITE

ACCESSORY: Wings

LIKES: Changing from a
caterpillar into a butterfly

DISLIKES: Spiderwebs

FAVORITE FOOD: String beans

FAVORITE ACTIVITY: Stopping to smell the roses

BUNNY

EYE COLOR: Bright blue

BODY COLOR: Cream

FAVORITE ACCESSORY:
Magician's cape

LIKES: Magic tricks

DISLIKES: Disappearing

FAVORITE FOOD: Carrot soup

FAVORITE ACTIVITY: Being
pulled out of a hat

CAT

EYE COLOR: Grassy green

BODY COLOR: White

FAVORITE ACCESSORY: Scratching post

LIKES: Getting manicures

DISLIKES: Hangnails

FAVORITE FOOD: Tuna salad sandwiches

FAVORITE ACTIVITY: Chasing balls of yarn

MOUSE

EYE COLOR: Purple

BODY COLOR: Gray

FAVORITE ACCESSORY: Birthday hats

LIKES: Throwing parties

DISLIKES: When balloons pop

FAVORITE FOOD: Birthday cake

FAVORITE ACTIVITY: Blowing out candles

CAT

EYE COLOR: Light blue

BODY COLOR: Golden, white, and charcoal

FAVORITE ACCESSORY: Pink bow

LIKES: Wearing skirts

DISLIKES: The end of a good party

FAVORITE FOOD: Vanilla cupcakes with pink frosting

FAVORITE ACTIVITY: Being the hostess

PUG

EYE COLOR: Emerald

BODY COLOR: Tan

FAVORITE ACCESSORY: A goody bag

LIKES: Opening presents

DISLIKES: Forgetting to send thank-you cards

FAVORITE FOOD: Oatmeal cookies

FAVORITE ACTIVITY: Serving punch

KITTEN

EYE COLOR: Bright green

BODY COLOR: White and gray

FAVORITE ACCESSORY:
Sparkly red slippers

LIKES: Making new friends

DISLIKES: Being away from home

FAVORITE FOOD: Apple pie

FAVORITE ACTIVITY: Watching
The Wizard of Oz

KITTEN

EYE COLOR: Light blue

BODY COLOR: Gray

FAVORITE ACCESSORY:
Digital camera

LIKES: Photography

DISLIKES: When people
don't smile

FAVORITE FOOD: Strawberries

FAVORITE ACTIVITY: Taking
pictures of friends

PUPPY

EYE COLOR: Mossy green

BODY COLOR: Golden brown and white

FAVORITE ACCESSORY: Boom box

LIKES: Break-dancing

DISLIKES: Country music

FAVORITE FOOD: Granola bars

FAVORITE ACTIVITY: Entering dance competitions

SNAIL

EYE COLOR: Blue-green

BODY COLOR: Pink with green shell

FAVORITE ACCESSORY: Camping gear

LIKES: Bungee jumping

DISLIKES: Impatience

FAVORITE FOOD: Peanut brittle

FAVORITE ACTIVITY: Going on adventures

PUPPY

EYE COLOR: Purple

BODY COLOR: Dark brown and cream

FAVORITE ACCESSORY: Soccer ball

LIKES: Gym class

DISLIKES: Doing homework

FAVORITE FOOD: Cookies and milk

FAVORITE ACTIVITY: Recess

KITTEN

EYE COLOR: Pale blue

BODY COLOR: Golden brown and white

FAVORITE ACCESSORY:

Pom-poms

LIKES: Cheerleading

DISLIKES: Losing her voice

FAVORITE FOOD:

Potato chips

FAVORITE ACTIVITY:

Rooting for the home team

DOG

EYE COLOR: Purple-blue

BODY COLOR: Cream and tan

FAVORITE ACCESSORY:
Electronic organizer

LIKES: Being organized

DISLIKES: Messiness

FAVORITE FOOD: Ham
and cheese sandwiches

FAVORITE ACTIVITY:
Planning for the future

SPIDER

EYE COLOR: Lime green

BODY COLOR: Purple and pink

FAVORITE ACCESSORY:
A web

LIKES: Anything sticky

DISLIKES: Chasing dinner

FAVORITE FOOD: Whatever
drops in

FAVORITE ACTIVITY:
Watching horror movies

DACHSHUND

EYE COLOR: Green

BODY COLOR: Dark brown

FAVORITE ACCESSORY:
Plaid doggy bed

LIKES: Watching TV

DISLIKES: Commercials

FAVORITE FOOD: TV dinners

FAVORITE ACTIVITY: Channel surfing

YORKIE

EYE COLOR: Ice blue

BODY COLOR: Black and brown

FAVORITE ACCESSORY:
Rope chew toy

LIKES: Hanging out in the doghouse

DISLIKES: Being alone

FAVORITE FOOD: Steak

FAVORITE ACTIVITY:
Playing video games with friends

POODLE

EYE COLOR: Lime green
BODY COLOR: Cream
FAVORITE ACCESSORY: Mirror
LIKES: Getting her hair cut
DISLIKES: Tangles
FAVORITE FOOD: Strawberry milk shakes
FAVORITE ACTIVITY: Picking a new hairstyle

POODLE

EYE COLOR: Blue
BODY COLOR: Pink and white
FAVORITE ACCESSORY: Fashion magazines
LIKES: French art
DISLIKES: Outdoors
FAVORITE FOOD: French toast
FAVORITE ACTIVITY: Shopping in Paris

CAT

EYE COLOR: Emerald green
BODY COLOR: White
FAVORITE ACCESSORY: Fancy bed
LIKES: Fluffy pillows
DISLIKES: Crumbs in bed
FAVORITE FOOD: Paté
FAVORITE ACTIVITY: Eating breakfast in bed

These cute critters are the smartest pals around. They know all the best tricks and are ready to show off their talents!

BIRD

EYE COLOR: Violet

BODY COLOR: Turquoise and yellow

FAVORITE ACCESSORY: Telephone

LIKES: Chatting

DISLIKES: Missed calls

FAVORITE FOOD: Pumpkin seeds

FAVORITE ACTIVITY: Talking on the phone

HORSE

EYE COLOR: Pale blue

BODY COLOR: Golden and white

FAVORITE ACCESSORY: Pink saddle

LIKES: Prancing

DISLIKES: Surprises

FAVORITE FOOD: Sugar cookies

FAVORITE ACTIVITY: Galloping

HAMSTER

EYE COLOR: Blue-green

BODY COLOR: White and golden

FAVORITE ACCESSORY:
Hamster wheel

LIKES: Working out

DISLIKES: Laziness

FAVORITE FOOD: Pears

FAVORITE ACTIVITY: Flexing muscles

MOUSE

EYE COLOR: Bright blue

BODY COLOR: Pink

FAVORITE ACCESSORY:
Cell phone

LIKES: Being a caring friend

DISLIKES: Gossip

FAVORITE FOOD: Toast with jelly

FAVORITE ACTIVITY: Collecting marbles

MOUSE

EYE COLOR: Pink-purple

BODY COLOR: Pink

FAVORITE ACCESSORY:
Hamster wheel

LIKES: Fruit

DISLIKES: Vegetables

FAVORITE FOOD: Kiwis

FAVORITE ACTIVITY: Peeling oranges

MOUSE

EYE COLOR: Sky blue

BODY COLOR: Gray

FAVORITE ACCESSORY: Slide

LIKES: Playing video games

DISLIKES: Low scores

FAVORITE FOOD: Waffles

FAVORITE ACTIVITY:
Getting the highest score

GECKO

EYE COLOR:

Olive and brown

BODY COLOR:

Green with orange spots

FAVORITE ACCESSORY:

Necklace

LIKES: Playing hide-and-seek

DISLIKES: Being found

FAVORITE FOOD: Chinese

FAVORITE ACTIVITY: Changing colors

BUNNY

EYE COLOR: Light blue

BODY COLOR: Chocolate, brown, and white

FAVORITE ACCESSORY:

Skateboard

LIKES: Extreme sports

DISLIKES: Laziness

FAVORITE FOOD: Energy bars

FAVORITE ACTIVITY: Doing backflips

KITTEN

EYE COLOR: Deep blue

BODY COLOR:

Tan and cream

FAVORITE ACCESSORY:

Gym membership

LIKES: Running

DISLIKES: Being out of breath

FAVORITE FOOD: Protein shakes

FAVORITE ACTIVITY: Competing in triathlons

PUPPY

EYE COLOR: Periwinkle

BODY COLOR:

Tan, brown, and white

FAVORITE ACCESSORY:

Stroller

LIKES: Being taken for walks

DISLIKES: Touching the ground

FAVORITE FOOD:

Anything in a bottle

FAVORITE ACTIVITY: Being babied

OWL

EYE COLOR: Yellow-brown

BODY COLOR: Golden and tan

FAVORITE ACCESSORY: The moon

LIKES: Hooting

DISLIKES: Early mornings

FAVORITE FOOD: Midnight snacks

FAVORITE ACTIVITY: Flying at night

TOTALLY TWINS

Seeing double? These twins know that twice the pet means twice the love!

PANDA

EYE COLOR: Lavender

BODY COLOR:

Black and white

FAVORITE ACCESSORY:

MP3 player

LIKES: Hard rock

DISLIKES: Classical

FAVORITE FOOD: Stir-fry

FAVORITE ACTIVITY: Going to rock concerts

PANDA

EYE COLOR: Bright blue

BODY COLOR:

Black and white

FAVORITE ACCESSORY:

Violin

LIKES: Classical music

DISLIKES: Hard rock

FAVORITE FOOD: Fortune cookies

FAVORITE ACTIVITY: Playing the piano

How big is your Littlest Pet Shop™?
Check 'em out!